Oral sex

By Alexandr Master

Table of contents:

Blowjob: instructions for use

1. Why it is important to have oral sex skills

As a doctor who deals with problems in the sexual sphere, I regularly encounter women's inability and unwillingness to understand the nature of male arousal. Many of my patients are strongly convinced that all they need to do in bed is periodically moan and obediently spread their legs. However, in sex, partners have equal roles. And a woman, just like a man, must be able to give her beloved pleasure, or at least try to do so.

Very often, women of all ages do not think about the fact that the ability to do a good Blowjob is the main indicator of a good mistress. Because everyone can lie in bed in silence and give themselves to a partner without exception. This behavior does not require any experience or effort from you. But to give your man an incredible pleasure, deftly handling his penis with your lips – this is what only a few modern women can do.

Due to the General obsession with the emancipation of society, representatives of the fair sex are less and less set out to learn how to qualitatively meet the male need for sex. Most women think that pleasure in bed should be given exclusively to her, and a man will somehow manage. Moreover, women do not care much about the fact that they are completely worthless, do not know how to mistress, who can not even properly make a Blowjob to their man.

Is it any wonder that most couples, one way or another, soon find themselves in the office of a sexologist? After all, a man has the same equal right to receive sexual pleasure as a woman. And, without receiving any emotional and physical return, few of the stronger sex will not think about what it would be worth to have a mistress.

Blowjob is not only an opportunity to deliver an unforgettable sexual pleasure to your partner, it is also a chance to demonstrate your affection, love and trust. This is how the average man perceives oral sex – it is a special sexual and emotional connection with a partner, which sharpens all the sensory organs of the senses. This is why men love oral sex.

In addition, the woman's nature, whether she wants it or not, still has a pronounced instinct of submission. The desire to belong entirely to her partner and the desire for him to possess her body. The man, in turn, also wants to achieve his unlimited power over the partner in sex, so that oral sex satisfies the hidden urges of both lovers at the same time.

A good lover and caring loving woman will not allow her partner to get out of bed without making sure that he is 100% satisfied with their sexual relationship. After all, this will not only warm up the partner's interest in his person, but even keep him close to you.

A good lover, a man is always subconsciously afraid of losing, and even such women are more often and much more jealous. And, of course, a relaxed and skilled partner in bed is much less likely to change. You can trust me as a sexologist: even the most beautiful, but cold in bed woman will soon get tired of a man who is tired of her selfishness and unwillingness to show a reciprocal passion.

My office is very often visited by the husbands of women who do not want to express their violent attraction to a sexual partner. Men are offended that their wives never seek to satisfy them with oral sex, and if they do Blowjob, then with such a face, as if thinking: "If only it would end soon!" Naturally, men are not idiots, and they are perfectly aware and notice when their partner does not bring much pleasure in making love. This not only brings discord into the relationship of the couple, but also makes the offended partner hold a grudge. After all, we men so ardently strive to give the woman we love pleasure. So why does she take it for granted? And why isn't he eager to do the same for us?

The ability to make a good Blowjob is as important a quality for a woman as it is to cook well or give birth to children. Because this is exactly the point in the relationship of a couple, the presence of which significantly facilitates joint life and helps to avoid the extinction of mutual sexual attraction. I have long noticed that families in which a man and a woman regularly engage in oral sex are much stronger than those couples where the partner is not willing to make concessions to her man.

Also, oral sex and Blowjob, which you regularly do to your beloved man, will strengthen your union and prevent the loss of previous feelings. Because you will remain as close and open to each other as possible, despite the years spent together. Of course, the partner himself should want to satisfy his woman in all possible ways, including with the help of oral sex. However, practice shows that usually such problems do not occur on the male side. The reluctance to engage in oral sex in the vast majority of cases is shown by a woman.

This refusal is painfully perceived by a man. It seems to him that the beloved disdains him, has fallen out of love with him, has ceased to be interested in him as a sexual object. A lot of people complain that the partner is simply disgusted to do a Blowjob for some reason that the offended husband or boyfriend is not able to understand.

A patient of mine once got desperate by going on a citrus diet for more than a week to improve the taste of his sperm, and also used waxing strips to get rid of hair in the intimate area. However, even after such victims, the woman did not appreciate the efforts of her husband and continued to give him a Blowjob through the force, driving the unfortunate man more and more into a state of quiet depression.

In the end, tired of not being able to find a way to his woman's heart, the man came to my office with her. And then it turned out that his wife is not too eager to show a reciprocal passion for a partner. It is not surprising that such a selfish attitude hurt her loving husband very much.

Imagine that you are madly attracted to a person and want to spend the rest of your life with them. You do everything in your power to make this person feel good around you. But when it comes to bed, you notice with what a dissatisfied look the partner is having sex with you, and when asked to do "nice mouth" and does not hide his disgust or his reluctance. This is how a man understands a bad Blowjob, which is done through force just so that the partner finally falls behind.

Resentment, anger, irritation and frustration are feelings that sooner or later, having accumulated and reached the limit, will inevitably result in something bad. In fatigue from his cold woman, in infidelity, in the desire to separate, in the end.

Blowjob for a man is a special opportunity to prove to his partner that he fully possesses her and values her trust. And, according to recent research by American scientists, it is those couples in which both partners regularly satisfy each other with oral sex, there is harmony and mutual understanding.

In this book, you will not only find the answer to the question of how to learn to enjoy oral sex and enjoy the excitement of your partner, but also learn about the ten most important rules of Blowjob. They will help you to raise the level of your skills in bed and teach you to deliver a real pleasure to a man. So that you become an experienced, beautiful mistress, able to deftly manage the sexual arousal of your beloved man.

Even those women who usually willingly agree to oral sex with their partner, often make a number of serious mistakes. Modern women think that Blowjob is a simple occupation, and it is enough just to put the partner's penis in your mouth, that's all the task. Of course, this is not the case. In order to achieve a bright orgasm in a man, you will have to try, and at the same time apply techniques of oral sex, which not everyone knows about.

It is interesting: there is information about an ancient and secret cult that existed in China several tens of centuries ago. Young women preparing to get married were taught the secret knowledge of oral sex. It was believed that the main duty of a wife is to be able to satisfy the sexual needs of her husband. This was an important and mandatory skill, since a high-quality sex life made a man a seasoned and confident warrior.

Of course, women living in our days, this issue is not so much concerned. Despite the fact that giving each other pleasure and showing tenderness, love and care is the main task of both partners. Modern women do not tend to take care of their men, and this selfishness begins with the sexual sphere. Without getting the proper release and emotional intimacy in bed, men lose high motivation to achieve their goals, become passive and disappointed in life. It is not for nothing that they used to say in Mexico that a lazy husband is the fault of a cold wife. In other words, the role of female sexuality in a man's life plays a much larger role than we used to think.

If a partner feels loved and confident in their own sexual power, they will reason and behave more sensibly than a man who is regularly tormented by suspicions of his partner's lack of emotional attachment. Feeling a strong emotional connection with his woman, the representative of the stronger sex is literally ready to turn mountains, protecting his beloved and wanting to provide her with the most comfortable existence.

In fact, it is sex that helps to establish a close emotional relationship between two young people of different genders. And no other measure can strengthen love more than regular and high-quality sex, including oral sex.

This is explained logically from the point of view of science: both partners, stimulating the erogenous zones and intimate places of each other, get a "hormonal thrashing", in which a large amount of oxytocin enters the blood. It is this hormone that is responsible for getting used to and feeling attached to your partner. That is, frequent and good sex is really able to bring you closer to your man.

What is the role of the Blowjob itself in this? And here's the thing: during oral sex, a man's blood receives a much greater amount of " positive " hormones than during vaginal sex. A lot of this lies in the very secret feelings that I have already described above. This is pure male psychology – it is pleasant and important for the partner to realize that he has his own woman and he needs to get confirmation that she trusts him and does not feel a sense of disgust in front of him.

Doing a Blowjob to your husband or boyfriend, you seem to say to him: "I love you and adore every cell of your body, there is no one closer and more desirable than you."

2. Why women don't want to do blowjobs

There is nothing difficult about loving a Blowjob if you are a representative of the strong half of humanity. As for women, not all of them are wildly enthusiastic about this kind of sexual activity. Some simply do not like their partner and therefore they do not want to do a Blowjob, others do not like the taste of male lubricant, semen or just the natural smell of the genitals.

With the first category, I think, you do not need to deal with it for a long time. If you do not love your man at all and are disgusted with him, if there is no emotional connection between you (or at least a banal "spark"), then no advice will help you experience real excitement in bed. In this case, any tricks are useless.

However, in situations where a woman simply does not know how to do a Blowjob correctly or finds a man's fragrance not so tempting, you can and even need to help her. And I immediately want to note that many wives complain that their active sexual life is sometimes hindered by a sensitive sense of smell. They are not to blame for this – the beautiful half of humanity all the senses are sharper than men.

So even a clean and completely healthy sexual organ of a spouse or boyfriend can have a specific smell, which is difficult to get rid of. This is also normal. Sexually Mature people are distinguished by this special, barely perceptible smell that accumulates in the pubic area and armpits.

Nature intended this to attract members of the opposite sex, signaling the potential partner's ability to have sex and subsequent conception. It is unlikely that nature would have expected that as humanity progressed, it would have found natural things disgusting or vile. That we will begin to get rid of hair growing on the body or strive to destroy your natural body smell.

However, I have one small, but very effective advice for ladies who often suffer from increased squeamishness in sex or do not tolerate the taste and smell of the male penis. If you are excited enough, you will simply stop feeling the specific aroma coming from your sexual partner's pubis, and the not quite pleasant taste of his lubricant.

This is interesting: in the stage of increased sexual excitability, the woman's body begins to work somewhat differently, so that even the most acute sense of smell magically evaporates for a time, and the squeamishness recedes under the pressure of natural instincts.

So you can use this advice to stop suffering by giving a Blowjob to your favorite man. Just explain to your partner that you need to experience sexual arousal too, and therefore you will not refuse preliminary caresses. In the end, your partner will not be harmed if before a Blowjob he spends some ten or fifteen minutes on you to "wind up" you properly. You don't need to be a genius to guess – an excited woman will satisfy her partner much better than one who does it through force or without much enthusiasm.

You can " wind up " yourself before the upcoming Blowjob on your own, without resorting to the help of a man. It doesn't really matter. Many women like to masturbate while taking a bath or shower. A little relaxation before oral sex will help you tune in to the right feelings and allow you to feel the pleasure of this procedure, even if the partner does not caress you during the Blowjob process. Naturally, you should not bring yourself to an orgasm before a

Blowjob – it is better to stay "on edge", so as not to lose your sexual fervor.

Sometimes in the case of acute natural squeamishness of women, oral sex in the bathroom helps out. And for your partner, this can be a pleasant innovation and variety in sexual life, if you do not often make love outside of bed. Try to take a shower together or lie in the bath filled with fragrant foam, light candles and turn on your favorite music. First, caress the sensitive areas on the partner's body with your fingers and hands, and then move lower and use your tongue. Even if your sexual partner has a sharp and pronounced body odor, such a small trick will temporarily reduce the level of odorous enzymes located in the upper layers of his skin – they will simply wash out of the pores.

In addition, a banal diet can improve the smell and taste of the penis and male sperm. To do this, you should temporarily give up fatty, hard-to-digest and high-calorie food of animal origin, replacing the bulk of dishes. Baked vegetables and fresh fruit are good, and you should also ask your man to drink simple purified water as often as possible. Weak herbal diuretic decoctions, which, among other things, remove toxins from the body and skin cells, thereby improving the smell of the body and genitals, will also play into your hands.

However, I want to note that it is not necessary to openly declare the truth to your loved one that it is unpleasant to do a Blowjob. If a man takes care of his appearance and health, adheres to the rules of personal hygiene and does not have sexually transmitted infections, then a sharp or strong smell coming from his intimate areas is not pathological or abnormal. In other words, this is its natural feature.

Among other things, men with dark skin tone and dark thick hair are more likely to have a more pronounced aroma of the body and genitals than, for example, men with blond hair. However, neither of them is to blame. This is just a natural feature. Therefore, if you tell your partner that you do not want to have oral sex with him, you can seriously offend and even deeply hurt the feelings of your chosen one. Moreover, practice shows that such outspoken statements are very painful for a man, believing that a woman simply does not love him.

In General, in fact, in couples where there is mutual love and trust, such problems often do not occur. Having a strong attachment to each other, people want to give their partner as much sexual pleasure as possible in bed, because the reluctance to engage in any type of sex simply does not occur. Therefore, a loving man never asks a loving woman to give him a Blowjob – she already knows perfectly well what and when her partner wants.

If you really intend to maintain your relationship or, even more so, marriage, then you will have to reconsider your views on sexual life in your union, because even a small sexual dissatisfaction can develop into large-scale problems of a completely unexpected nature.

If both you and your man are still at a fertile age, then sex is a thing whose quality and frequency will inevitably affect your relationship and even the depth of feelings for each other. Therefore, you will have to, one way or another, become an ideal lover for your spouse or boyfriend and learn to do Blowjob correctly, and even love this occupation no less than your partner.

As I have already indicated above, much of this depends on the sexual mood of the woman herself. If you literally start making a Blowjob to your favorite man from the threshold, without reaching the proper level of sexual desire, then this action is very unlikely to bring you any pleasure.

Both you and your partner should be aware that any sex is an occupation for both of you, and therefore your feelings should also be taken into account. Therefore, if your man is serious about getting his portion of pleasure, do not hesitate to tell him that this is a game for two. Only after you get excited enough, the partner can count on a great Blowjob, but not before.

I also want to highlight the male errors that often appear in the field of oral sex, which makes a woman lose all interest in it. Some men naively believe that a woman is obliged to give them pleasure at the first click of her fingers, while her personal feelings are not so important. However, the task of a good lover is not to force his lady to do what she absolutely does not want, but to make her want it herself.

Therefore, the man himself should take the initiative, at least at the initial stage of the prelude preceding the Blowjob. And you have a full and legal right to refuse your partner and even be offended if he is not going to even think about your return pleasure.

If your partner requires a Blowjob, then he must bring you to orgasm – before, during oral sex, or after. Some couples prefer to perform oral sex "alternately" in order to enjoy the sensations and excitement of their partner to the full. That is, first, for example, the initiative is shown by the woman, and then, when the man has reached sexual discharge, it is his turn to fulfill his part of the unspoken obligations.

This does not necessarily have to be a response to oral sex. A man can just make love to you, or maybe you want something else, or he will simply satisfy you with the help of his "deft fingers". The point here is different: if only one of you gets pleasure and the other doesn't, it weakens your emotional connection. In the end, it is even just humanly ugly and selfish.

This is why in situations where a man regularly requires oral sex, without bothering to respond to his partner and without caring about how to satisfy her sexual need, he eventually comes across a woman's reluctance to do Blowjob at all.

If such a moment occurs regularly in your couple, you should talk openly with your partner and explain to him that leaving you "with nothing" is rude and wrong. And that you also have the right to count on your portion of "sweet sensations" if you have made a Blowjob.

And I will even say more – if you regularly satisfy your boyfriend, but after a Blowjob, sexual contact will end, and you will not experience an orgasm, it will undermine your mutual feelings for each other. The fact is that even without realizing it, a woman subconsciously perceives actions of this sexual nature as devoid of love and humiliating for her self-esteem. This is why in the future, having experienced this feeling repeatedly and secretly (and often without even knowing it), she may experience negative emotions and even disgust every time a partner starts talking about a Blowjob. And in this case, the man is solely to blame.

In the same cases, when a man cares about the enjoyment of his beautiful woman, a Blowjob will be perceived by her as a prelude to her own orgasm. Subconsciously, a woman will not feel any internal discomfort or feelings of rejection, because she will be sure that the man will make sure that she is as good as he is now, even if she is doing a Blowjob, without receiving a response at this very moment.

In such situations, the principle always applies: "I do well for you, and you will do well for me!". And because a woman is able to experience great pleasure and pleasure, satisfying her man with oral sex.

Thus, not in every couple, the unwillingness or inability of a woman to give a Blowjob to her lover means a problem on her part. Rude and selfish behavior of a man can alienate the partner, forcing her to lock herself in bed and refuse to play "one-man show". And you can't blame her for that.

However, we have forgotten about another category of women – those who have no reason to refuse oral sex, or unwillingness to do it. It is for them that I will give a detailed diagram of how ideally a Blowjob should be performed, so that it brings maximum pleasure to both partners. In other words, I will tell you how to become the perfect mistress for your partner, if you are banal do not know how to do Blowjob.

Blowjob: instructions for use

3. Rule one: you have to like yourself

In the nature of any woman, no matter how she looks and no matter how old she is, there is one simple, but ardent desire – to be attractive. This desire also guides a woman's behavior at the moment of intimacy with a man. In other words, for the fair sex, what they look like during sex is of the most important importance. And whether they remain attractive in the eyes of men.

In order to relax and enjoy a Blowjob, it is important for a woman to start this action fully armed. This will allow you to drive away unnecessary thoughts and even to achieve self-excitation. If you are sure that you look incredibly sexy and attractive, then your partner's sexual arousal will be transmitted to you. This is why it is important to prepare a little before going to bed with a loved one.

By the way, my old friend Patricia, with whom we have been friends since College, does exactly this. Despite the fact that she has been the wife of her husband for ten years and the mother of two charming girls, her sexual life with her husband still reigns former passion. The answer to this phenomenon is very simple: Patricia always spends some time in front of the mirror before appearing in front of her husband in bed. And she is 100% sure that she looks amazing, and therefore she is happy to demonstrate not only her body, but also the desire to give her husband sexual pleasure.

In addition to the fact that Patricia does not suffer from excessive shyness and coldness in bed, she also supports the sexual interest of her husband in her person. Periodically, she changes her makeup and hairstyle, creating the illusion of novelty, which is so necessary for most men. Patricia says that even a single unusual detail can make a man look at her in a new way - hungry and absorbing every inch of her body with his eyes.

At the same time, nothing so pretentious Patricia never invents. So, according to her, once she simply tied a silk scarf around her neck, while remaining completely naked. This item of clothing created a rather strange, but exciting feeling, bringing a certain dissonance to the familiar and familiar image of the wife.

And on one of the stormy nights of their marriage, Patricia used old torn tights that she had specially holed in the most interesting place. The effect was stunning – her husband could not calm down for a long time, getting used to the pedantic and overly neat wife, now flaunted in such a stunning form.

My friend's secret is simple enough: she takes the time to be completely satisfied with her reflection in the mirror. She says that she has long noticed this relationship – if she finds her reflection in the mirror especially attractive, it seems to open up in bed, which makes their sex with her husband especially sensual and passionate.

In fact, it's really important. It is unlikely that you will be able to give a Blowjob to your favorite man with a calm soul, if you are concerned that today you do not look as tempting as usual. Such negative thoughts and negative emotions can spoil the sexual atmosphere that reigns around, and at the same time give rise to a variety of complexes.

Perhaps someone will find it rather stupid to preen before having sex with a partner. But that's what you women did once, in the past, isn't it? When you went out on a date, you carefully applied makeup, curled your eyelashes and styled your hair, taking out the most beautiful and sexy dress from the closet. And they realized that all this makes you much more beautiful and attractive in the eyes of men, and therefore – in their own.

The desire to continue to look good and enjoy your own reflection in the mirror is an important trait even after fifteen years of marriage. Although, rather, this is an especially important trait if your relationship has already gone for years.

By emphasizing your femininity and your natural essence along with your desire to remain desirable (no matter how beautiful you are, this is just a small thing), you also emphasize that you remain, first of all, a woman next to your man. Not his wife, not a housewife or mother of children, but a female who is still driven by the desire to arouse the interest of the opposite sex.

By reading your mood, a man will unconsciously adopt your behavior model, striving to remain a male to satisfy your natural instincts. All this helps maintain the fire of passion and keep the storm between you from subsiding and fading, because you do not forget about your original, even lower, nature.

Feeling beautiful and feminine, you will be in a pleasant sexual excitement and expectation that you will soon be possessed by a man. And then a Blowjob that can bring him to a nervous shiver, will bring no less pleasure to you yourself.

Female sexuality begins in the head, arising from thoughts, feelings, and even fantasies. A woman is the personification of passion and lust, and she is looking for a partner who is ready to accept and implement this passion in real life. That is, the quality of sex in the marital bed will always depend on the woman, on her self-confidence, on her perception of her own sensuality and beauty.

If you are confident and ready to open up, once in the hands of a man, he will immediately respond to your behavior. This is why the same partner can be completely different with two women. On the one hand, a man can be passive in bed and personify a bad and inattentive lover. On the other hand, he is able to radically change his behavior in bed, becoming an ideal and hot lover.

In fact, a man is just a "reagent" to female sexuality. And if you have too little of this sexuality, it is almost certain that your partner will not be able to "get through" to her.

Therefore, do not strive to become desirable for your man in the first place. This is a big and gross mistake. Strive to become sexy and luxurious for yourself. And then you will not have to convince your man that you are beautiful and sexy.

Let yourself be what you want. Only if you feel internally confident in your own femininity and attractiveness, you will be able to get real pleasure in bed with your partner. Even when you satisfy his sexual need and make a Blowjob.

4. The second rule: a man should like you

The first rule should be logically supplemented with the second, but everything is much simpler here. Pleasing a man is not as difficult as it may seem to women. In fact, representatives of the strong half of humanity are not so picky about beauty and are not as demanding as people think. And inventing complex methods of seduction does not make sense.

Rather, the main task of a woman is to catch what exactly makes her man excited. If in the female world with this all can be very difficult and confusing, then with men you can not break your head. All their secret (as it seems to them) desires always remain on the surface. And yet they are insanely, just obscenely simple and even primitive.

In fact, to excite your partner to the maximum, a woman needs only two things: to collect in your image those items that represent female sexuality for him, and at the same time and like yourself (this point we have already discussed above).

It doesn't take much for an ordinary man to feel a rush of unprecedented excitement. For example, you can please him by making his favorite hairstyle or painting his nails bright red varnish, if he comes from this indescribable delight.

And even better – to do everything at once to be the living embodiment of his dreams and sexual fantasies. Since the stronger sex really likes eyes, it will not be difficult to give them aesthetic pleasure. You, like no one else, know what turns your partner on and likes it the most.

So, if he loves loose hair flowing over bare shoulders, and believes that you look as attractive as possible in this image, then you do not need to think long about how to make an unforgettable impression on him. Just let your hair fall down your back.

If he finds it sexy to see a naked woman with high heels on her legs, then wear high-heeled shoes before coming to the bedroom. In General, as a sexologist, I can confidently say that any sexual desire of a man can be made a reality in a few moments. Because usually it is just a collection of some little things. For example, the same aforementioned heels, lush loose curls or red lipstick combined with lacy black panties.

If your partner doesn't have any clear preferences and requirements for female appearance (or you haven't had time to calculate them), then you can always choose something neutral – something that most men like. So, many people like to watch their partner become a depraved and bad girl. You can emphasize your "availability" in bed with suitable underwear or even just unusual behavior.

One of my patients, for example, was wildly delighted every time his wife put on ordinary white panties, which she moved slightly to the side so that the area of her perineum was visible. Such a small thing drove him to sexual frenzy, because it seemed to him a model of sex appeal and female vulgarity. And one of my long-time male patients didn't have to wait too long to please – just put on plain nylon stockings.

I want to say that despite the true belief that all men love with their eyes, these same eyes are not looking for something so extraordinary. Therefore, in order to bring your partner to a bright and powerful orgasm, you do not need to puzzle over what to come up with.

However, I still want to give readers some effective tips that I learned from my long-term practice as a family sexologist. These small tricks will help you if you need to spur the sexual interest of your partner or if you want to make a Blowjob a truly unforgettable event.

First of all, try the effect of a sharp change in temperature. The head of the male penis is a very sensitive area of the body that reacts not only to touch, but also to humidity and temperature. Therefore, ordinary ice cubes will help you make a high-class Blowjob.

The temperature of the oral cavity in women usually ranges between 37 degrees Celsius, while frozen water has a temperature below zero. Such a sharp contrast of sensations can not only surprise and provoke a man, but also allow him to feel new, more vivid sexual experiences. In addition, this "game of temperatures" well stimulates the power of ejaculation. That's why a man's orgasm after such a Blowjob will always be brighter than without this technique.

If you are passionate about becoming your man's dream lover and the most desirable woman in the universe, then learn to be a little crazy. Men like it when a woman's behavior in bed is impossible to predict. If you suddenly, without any preliminaries, find your partner in a dark corner and pull down his pants, then he is unlikely to ever forget such a Blowjob simply because it will be a complete surprise for him.

Almost all men, without exception, like things that represent female sex appeal. These include short tight skirts, beautiful and sexy underwear, stockings and heels, bright makeup. So, you can save in your closet an ultra-short skirt and high uncomfortable heels especially for home sex games. This simple image is guaranteed to make a Blowjob more sensual for your partner, because it will emphasize your feminine essence and remind him that you are primarily a female.

5. Rule three: don't make a Blowjob in the dark

Above, I have already indicated the fact that a man really loves with his eyes, and therefore it is not necessary to hide oral caresses from him and hide them in the dark. A good lover, on the contrary, tries to emphasize what is happening, giving her partner the opportunity to observe her and see well everything that she does with him.

It is easy to guess that for a man to watch the body and face of a mistress making a Blowjob is a real pleasure. This not only allows him to feel, among other things, aesthetic pleasure, but also maintains the maximum level of arousal, which is why Blowjob seems so pleasant to a man.

In the early 2000s, an interesting test was conducted in the United States. Four married couples were asked to perform oral sex in separate rooms of a comfortable hotel. At the same time, the two couples were left in dark rooms without any lighting, since they were not allowed to turn on electricity during the experiment, and the windows were tightly curtained.

The remaining couples, on the other hand, were placed in rooms that were brightly lit with electric lights. At the end of the experiment, each couple was asked to rate the degree of their sexual arousal and the strength of their subsequent orgasm on a five-point scale. It turned out that those couples who performed oral sex in complete darkness did not rate the incident higher than three points. At the same time, the spouses who engaged in oral sex in the light were completely satisfied with the sexual contact and rated the resulting orgasm on the maximum scale.

Thus, it is important to observe the sexual process not only for a man, but also for a woman. This allows you to control the partner's reaction and change the tempo and rhythm of movements in time to give each other more pleasure. In addition, visualizing the sex process helps you feel more aroused than when you can't see anything and can't distinguish the outline of the partner's body in the dark and observe their sexual organs.

This may seem a little primitive for modern man, but the desire to watch and see the process of copulation dates back to the most ancient times, when it really was of great importance for the quality of female fertilization.

And let now the main meaning of visual contact in the process of sex has already been lost, but it is still impossible to exclude its aesthetic component. Men actually love to watch their partner give them a Blowjob, and there is no point in denying this harmless desire to their chosen one. On the contrary, if you want to give him more pleasure and become an ideal lover, it is better to forget about oral sex in the pitch dark forever. Even if you are self-conscious about your body or you are hindered by some complexes.

In favor of "illuminated Blowjob", as funny as it may sound, I will give another important argument, which will be difficult to argue with. If you can see your partner's face and body clearly while having sex, you will feel more emotionally attached to them and more satisfied after sex than if you were doing it in the dark. Because not being able to observe what is happening between the two of you creates a feeling of slight frustration and even sexual dissatisfaction. This is why men don't like having sex in the dark. They want to see their partner well, especially if she makes a Blowjob.

If you are too shy or feel insecure in the rays of bright light, you can always turn on a dim

lamp or light a few candles nearby.
However, I would like to note that,
according to recent research in the field of
human sexology, one interesting discovery
has been revealed: couples who often engage
in oral sex during the day, consider
themselves happier than those who indulge
in carnal pleasures exclusively in the dark.

Here I want to make a small digression and
explain why this is happening. The fact that
man is by his nature the creature of the day.
Our genotype has long been based on the
desire to stay awake in the daytime and sleep
at night. Our forefathers thus avoided the
attacks of nocturnal predators and increased
their chances of a long earth existence. This
instinct has remained strong to this day.

This means that with the onset of darkness,
our entire body begins to gradually prepare
for sleep, and its susceptibility to external
pathogens naturally decreases. For this
reason, morning or afternoon sex will always

be more sensual than night sex. And for the same reason, a Blowjob that you gave your man in the light of day will bring him a brighter orgasm than if you decided to postpone this activity until nightfall.

In addition, during the day, the human body works much more intensively, and blood pressure has higher indicators than at night. Therefore, not only the degree of arousal differs, but even its strength-the blood flows faster and more actively to the genitals in the daytime. But if you decide to have oral sex after midnight, then first you will have to " wake up " the partner's body.

Also, many of my colleagues-sexologists convince (based on a number of medical data) that Blowjob and oral sex is an occupation that takes place exclusively in the morning. Then sexual discharge will not just bring a man a sense of complete satisfaction, but also cause a rush of warm feelings for his mistress, who gave a bright and pleasant experience.

Of course, I do not want to convince you that it is necessary to give a Blowjob to a man only in the morning or at lunch. However, if you notice that you persistently do not enjoy this process or you are not doing it well, then it makes sense to try to do it in the light of day. Perhaps your body (or your partner's body) simply refuses to perform its sexual function at night. And so the quality of the sexual relationship suffers, and the excitement comes late, and even then not fully.

By the way: if you notice that the partner is not eager to watch you and generally prefers to keep his eyes closed while you do a Blowjob, then this is not a good sign. Most often, this behavior of a man signals that he is not too attached to you. Sometimes during oral sex, a man closes his eyes to fantasize about other women.

6. Rule four: posture matters

Bed is not a place for complexes and prejudices, but women are often simply ashamed to take a frank position when engaged in oral sex. Especially if the relationship with your partner started recently and the embarrassment still hasn't completely disappeared.

However, the more frank and depraved your pose will be during oral sex, the more pleasure the man will get. Ideally, during a Blowjob, to achieve the greatest excitement, you need to use two types of positions: those in which the partner gets the opportunity to observe your face and those that open access to your genitals.

In the first case, the classic positions in which the woman is at the feet of a man, and her face is turned towards his face, are perfect. This pose is also convenient in that it can be varied as it is convenient for both of you. You can do a Blowjob on your knees while the partner is standing with his legs straight; you can also lie down on the bed, taking a more comfortable, horizontal position; and this position allows you to do a Blowjob sitting down.

At the same time, in any of its varieties, a man gets the opportunity to watch the face of his mistress, as well as to see how his penis plunges into her mouth. This constantly keeps sexual arousal at a high level, in addition, many men like this position due to its aesthetic component. Who of the stronger sex does not want to watch how the beloved woman caresses him with her lips and tongue, closing her eyes with pleasure?

However, this common position has a very significant drawback – the partner loses the ability to fondle you or engage in oral sex with you in response. Moreover, he doesn't even always have the ability to reach your breasts to even stroke your nipples. Therefore, for women who need to get responses to stay aroused, this option is not suitable at all.

The second category of poses that are perfectly suitable for a Blowjob has this advantage: the partner can not only easily reach your sacred places to caress you or masturbate you while you are doing a Blowjob, if desired, he can also give you back oral caresses at any time. However, you can't watch your partner's face any more than they can watch yours. That is, the opportunity to enjoy his reaction to your caresses is lost.

Despite the fact that each couple independently chooses the most suitable position for a Blowjob, I still believe that the ideal solution is poses that leave room for action on the part of the man. One way or another, he will have to take care of the partner's satisfaction, because in the case when oral sex is delayed, the mistress may simply have time to get tired or lose her sexual fuse. Therefore, many women need to be helped to stay "on edge".

If you are going to have oral sex with your partner, try to be at the side of his thighs. So that he can simultaneously see your face and observe your actions, experiencing strong sexual arousal, and at the same time have the opportunity to caress you with his hands and fingers, if he wants to. This position optimally suits both partners, because there is no obvious disregard for the needs of the woman.

In addition, at a time of strong sexual tension, a man most often seeks not to enjoy the caress in proud solitude, but to show a response and satisfy his woman. This is a natural need that encourages the stronger sex to take care of the sexual satisfaction of their beloved woman.

Despite the fact that most men like to start enjoying oral sex first, in the process of Blowjob, the needs change dramatically, and the partner wants to have access to the sexual organs of his mistress. Therefore, even if your loved one never asks you about it and you usually do a Blowjob without getting a response, try to change your behavior a little. Stay in such a position that the man can always be near your erogenous zones. Most often, a loving partner will not resist, and eventually will want to caress you, or a Blowjob will develop into mutual oral sex.

By the way, I advise young women to think seriously if a man almost never shows a reciprocal interest in you during the Blowjob process. If such behavior happens rarely and in exceptional cases, it can not be considered a signal of a lack of spiritual attachment.

But in the case when the partner regularly asks to satisfy him orally, while not showing any activity in your direction, this can threaten very real problems in your relationship.

As I have already indicated above, it is rare for a man to refrain from trying to please his beloved woman during the Blowjob process. The desire to satisfy a woman lies in the psychology of any man who truly loves her.

In fact, your partner's behavior during a Blowjob can be more eloquent than any words. Often it is men's coldness and selfishness that discourage any desire for ladies to engage in this thankless occupation. After all, a man gets pleasure without caring about the feelings of his partner. Such "sexual indifference" in the process of Blowjob can really indicate a lack of love on the part of a man. Because, as I mentioned above, the desire to satisfy your woman is a natural need of a loving male. Even if he wants to get sexual pleasure first.

In short, if you suspect that your partner is using you, don't miss the opportunity to use the trick I described above. If even this measure does not cause your man to respond and want to caress you, then no one will dare to blame you for the fact that you do not like to do Blowjob.

7. Rule five: act consistently

Now I want to move on to a short but concise guide. So that a woman can imagine how to actually do a Blowjob. After all, many of the beautiful ladies think that all you need is just to put your partner's penis in your mouth.

In fact, even an inept mistress can bring a man to orgasm with oral sex. However, it is important to indicate one detail, which, unfortunately, is still not known by all women.

Conventionally, male discharge can be divided into" mechanical orgasm " and "emotional orgasm". Of course, in science, these things are called different terms and they look more complicated, but I will not complicate and explain everything much simpler.

Probably, any woman knows that a man reaches ejaculation under the influence of mechanical action – the friction of the glans of the penis. Therefore, many people think that nothing more needs to be done. A man can experience an orgasm when stimulating the penis with his hands, and during oral sex, and all other types of sexual intercourse. All this instills false confidence in the mind of women that all that is necessary for a partner is to squeeze his penis tighter and move the lips up and down.

Yes, this way you will actually bring your lover to ejaculation, but it will not be a quality orgasm, but just a mechanical effect. In the literal sense, under the influence of friction, the "valves" of the male body drain the seminal fluid into the ducts. This is how the male orgasm occurs. And you can bring a man to it very quickly, if you act actively – this is pure biology. That's just to emotional discharge and sexual, real sexual satisfaction, this will not lead to. That is, despite the fact that your man will finish, he will almost certainly not be happy with it. Why?

And here's the thing: in addition to the fact that a man's body is controlled by hormones and natural processes, he also has emotional needs and even a love attachment. This may seem wild, but a man's arousal also comes from his head, just like women's. Despite the fact that it is much easier to cause mechanical arousal in a man than in a woman.

In other words, you can't just put your penis in your mouth if you want to give your partner a moment of sexual bliss. This will only lead to a reflex orgasm that has very little to do with real and high-quality sexual discharge.

In modern society, a lot of books are written about women's sexuality and its complex natural nature, while men are given a very modest place. For this reason, most modern women simply do not imagine that a man wants all the same things that they themselves do.

A good Blowjob differs from a bad one in that the mistress skillfully "starts" her partner, gradually bringing him to a real sexual exhaustion and frenzy. This is a real subtle, but at the same time simple game that anyone can learn if they want.

If you set out to learn how to do a high-class Blowjob to please your man, then start acting slowly and consistently. First there are preliminary caresses that set up the partner for further sexual bliss. You should caress the man with your hands and fingers, gently descending to his intimate places, and not immediately cling to the penis with a death grip. Keep the intrigue and increase the desire of a man, slowly, time after time pushing the boundaries of what is allowed.

Only after the introduction in the form of tactile caresses and sliding strokes, you can go to light kisses and gradually fall into the area of the partner's perineum. But even now there is no need to hurry, otherwise the magic of gradually increasing sexual impatience will simply dissipate. First, do not go further than ordinary kisses, carefully avoiding the penis itself.

After you understand that it is not necessary to torment your partner, use the tongue to move to a new level of the game. Slid the tongue over the skin of the partner, gradually moving to his penis, and when you get to it, then start caressing from the bottom, from the base of the penis, and only then lightly touch the head with your tongue.

The most recent, final stage is the direct immersion of the male penis into the mouth. At the same time, there is no need to hurry. First, make your movements light, gliding, almost imperceptible. Do not submerge a man's penis deeper than the head. And, as you increase the density of the circumference of the lips, go lower and lower, capturing more and more of the length of the penis with your mouth.

This gradual, smooth beginning of the Blowjob will allow a man to experience a new range of emotions and feel a pleasant, exciting impatience. The partner will literally burn with the desire to quickly experience the next stage of your actions, and when you finally start oral sex, it will really bring him not just mechanical excitement, but real emotional pleasure.

After all, the mechanism of male sexuality is not as simple as most women believe. And do not confuse high-quality, emotional male orgasm, similar to an explosion, with banal mechanical ejaculation, which is not able to bring a deep sense of satisfaction at all.

A few years ago, a married couple in their middle years came to my office frequently. The reason for the visits was simple to the point of banality – the man was not satisfied with his sexual life with his wife. At the same time, the woman herself was perplexed why her life partner generally has these offensive claims, because he regularly ends up in the process of sex.

It never occurred to her that a man needs something more than a minute of active Blowjob, in which it is simply impossible to have time to get emotional discharge. After all, a man's body will automatically "discharge" before he has time to experience real sexual bliss.

When women who don't understand such simple and obvious things come to my office, the same question comes to mind – why is the beautiful half of humanity so strongly convinced that being a good lover literally means simply causing the release of sperm from your partner? After all, this is absolutely not true.

Obviously, many modern women are satisfied with this position, because it is very convenient for them. While a man sweats to please his beloved partner, a woman considers her duty fulfilled without doing anything at all. And few of these women will think about the fact that her partner can even finish with a vacuum cleaner. But it's not the same, is it?

8. Rule six: use both hands

Very often men complain to me that their wives and girlfriends simply do not want to be active during oral sex, and literally every action the unfortunate have to beat out, insistently begging the woman.

For example, an inexperienced mistress will almost never use her hands and palms in the process of Blowjob, because it seems superfluous and even completely unnecessary to her. She is deeply convinced that the erogenous zone on the body of a man is only one – this is the head of the penis. And if it is at this moment in the partner's mouth, then nothing more should be done.

Some women are genuinely perplexed when I tell them that, for example, the inner part of a man's thighs is no less sensitive than their own skin. Or that the surface of the male buttocks is an area that is worth stroking or even biting with your teeth to give your partner more pleasure. Or even that the testicles are not only a place of increased sensitivity, but also a zone of the body that responds perfectly to affection.

In fact, most modern men have no idea what a woman's caress or sexual tenderness is, because their mistresses are not interested in anything but the penis. But imagine what would happen in the world of beautiful ladies if men stopped caressing women's breasts, thighs, neck, tender tummy area and other sacred places. And they would be interested exclusively in the area of the female vagina, stubbornly not touching all other places.

Despite the fact that every living person of any gender has its own special places of hypersensitivity, yet nature has a large accumulation of nerve endings in individual areas of the skin, which occur in every woman and every man. In the latter category, such sacred areas on the body are, at least, the area of the anus, the base of the penis and the testicles.

While you are completely occupied with the head of your partner's penis, you have free hands that can and should be used to give a man additional pleasure. In this case, one of the palms is better placed on the base of the penis, tightly clasping it and moving your hand in time with your movements with your lips. This will increase the pleasant sensations and allow you to use a large area of the male sexual unit, especially if it has an impressive length or you can not put it in your mouth even half.

The second hand should be occupied with caressing the erogenous zone – for example, gently stroking the male testicles with it, or even wrapping your hand around them, without squeezing too hard, so as not to hurt the man. Most of the representatives of the stronger sex come to a real sexual ecstasy, when in addition to a banal Blowjob, their body also feels pleasant movements in the area of another part of the body.

In this case, the testicles can not only be touched with your fingers and stroked with your palm, but also gently caressed with your mouth, as well as the penis. If this area of your partner's body has a high threshold of sensitivity (and this is almost always the case), then the man will feel no less delight from these actions than from an ordinary Blowjob.

Moreover, as a variety, you can put a man's testicle in your mouth (choosing the one you like best) and gently suck it, while simultaneously masturbating the man with your hands. Very often, such a simple trick helps a man to feel an incredibly powerful orgasm.

As I mentioned above, the area of the anus also has a high degree of sensitivity, and therefore massage of this place can enhance sexual sensations during oral sex. It is not necessary to dip a finger inside the male anus if the partner does not want to. After all, not everyone will like this dubious pleasure. In addition, you can inadvertently hurt your partner with careless movements (or even injure the sensitive wall of the intestine with sharp nails). Most often, ordinary gentle sliding strokes are enough. At the same time, you should start with the buttocks – squeeze them and massage them, moving smoothly and slowly to the anal ring.

Even light movements around this area can be enough to make the partner feel good. And for some, it is enough to caress the skin of the buttocks. In short, experiment to find both hands work while you make your favorite man a Blowjob.

If the partner does not mind, during oral sex, a finger can be inserted inside the anus (of course, pre-lubricated with a special tool to facilitate sliding) or even an anal stimulator. Since the prostate is located in the anus of a man – the most sensitive place in the body, its stimulation can significantly increase the duration and strength of your partner's orgasm. In combination with simultaneous stimulation of the male penis, this promises an amazing emotional experience, but not every partner is ready to go to such experiments. Therefore, do not show excessive arrogance and diligence.

In short, it is very stupid to limit yourself exclusively to the head of the penis, making a Blowjob. A woman who really wants to satisfy her man and give him maximum sensations in bed, will never mindlessly pull the penis of the chosen one with her mouth, forgetting about other erogenous zones.

9. Rule seven: show that you like it too

Yes, I will return to this topic again – it is important for every loving man to know that his partner enjoys sexual contact with him, whatever it may be.

There is no surer way to bring a partner to ecstasy than showing how good you feel about what you do with him. If a man sees that you are exhausted from sexual desire, making him a Blowjob, it is better than chemical pills will sharpen all his feelings and bring to such lust that he will lose control of himself.

I do not encourage women to imitate violent ecstasy or pretend to moan, depicting animal passion, but to give a loved man a Blowjob with a stone face is the height of stupidity and even disrespect for the partner.

Subconsciously, any man wants to get in bed confirmation that he is able to give his woman pleasure and that she is happy, in turn, to possess his penis.

Try to show the man that you like what you do. That you actually experience sexual arousal and enjoy the process as much as he does. And if this is too difficult for you, you can always call on your own hands and help yourself to achieve arousal through Masturbation. Many men like it even more, and others may be encouraged to respond.

The realization that the partner is excited and fervently wants her man makes him completely happy and helps to feel a better sexual discharge.

In my practice, there was a case when the sex life of two young people went down just because the girl did not show signs of her arousal, although she liked to have sex with her boyfriend. It was just that she was a reserved and timid person who rarely gave vent to her emotions.

As a result, the unfortunate guy soon convinced himself that his partner did not want him and that she was bored and uninterested in bed with him. These doubts and suspicions soon developed into real complexes, and the frequency of sexual intercourse in this couple was reduced to a minimum.

The most painful for a man was oral sex – he was desperate to find signs of pleasure on the face of his girlfriend when she gave him a Blowjob, but it was not possible for him. The girl, in turn, decided that the sudden reluctance of the partner to have sex with her was caused by her inexperience and the fact that she stopped exciting him. As a result, both held a grudge against each other and refused to have sex.

This situation seems absurd enough, but in real life, much smaller problems can ruin a couple's sex life. I have already mentioned in the chapters above that it is extremely important for a man to be sure that a woman is comfortable with him and does not disdain him. So, a Blowjob is a kind of litmus test for the strong half of humanity, which allows you to identify any problems in sexual relations.

If a woman persists in remaining cold while performing oral sex, this will cause an unpleasant sediment in the soul of her partner.

I can also remember an interesting case related to this topic that occurred before I started my medical practice as a teenager, I had a best friend and sworn friend, Henry, with whom we literally shared all our personal experiences. Henry had a beautiful girlfriend - beautiful and slender, with an enviably feminine figure. Needless to say, Henry kept an eye on her, loved her to distraction, and was jealous of everything.

However, this relationship was not destined to migrate to adulthood. One day, Henry said in a desperate voice that he had made the decision to break up with his girlfriend. The reason was as tragic as it was funny – it seemed to him that the girl was dissatisfied with the size of his penis. When I asked him why he made such hasty conclusions, he said that the ex-girlfriend does not feel any visible excitement when having sex. That he had never heard her moan in bed, or even let him know in any other way that she was well.

But what offended Henry most of all was that each time during the Blowjob, the girl's face took on a distant look and she seemed completely indifferent. Wanting to get a storm of passion in response, Henry each time encountered only female sexual coldness, and the behavior of his partner during the Blowjob aggravated his fears.

Of course, now Henry is a successful doctor and a wise man, who would hardly have already started to follow the lead of men's resentments and complexes. However, this situation demonstrates very well how much can depend on a woman's behavior in bed. Because a man, unwittingly, notices literally everything, reading any emotions from the face of his beloved partner.

And if you want to maintain a relationship and regularly please your partner with your sexual abilities, take care of the need to enjoy the process with him. Because if a man truly loves you, he will expect from you both stifled sighs and muffled moans, despite what you do in bed. This is our nature.

By the way, now Henry is happily married to his former classmate. And although she is not as stunningly beautiful and slender as his youthful first love, nevertheless, she gives Henry what his masculine nature needs – an undisguised sexual desire and involvement

in this very process, from which both get
exactly what they crave.

10. Rule eight: sometimes prepare him for a blow job in advance

Sometimes we are not so much happy with the things themselves as with the anticipation of them. And this is a great opportunity to establish a sexual atmosphere in your relationship and even return to the former passion, if you have been living together for a very long time.

Very good for warming up a partner are frank and "dirty" correspondence, as well as erotic photos that you can throw at him while he is in the office or going home after work.

Men's psychology is somewhat different from women's, and this can be used for their own good, to maintain a high sensuous interest in their own person. Blowjob is the best gift that you can think of for a man, and if this gift is also promised, wrapped in a beautiful wrapper, you can count on the fact that the partner will come to ecstasy long before the event itself.

At the same time, many things that do not excite him in real life can have a stunning effect outside the walls of the house, as it turns into a real erotic game. That's why a nude photo of you sent to him via personal correspondence can make a real splash, even if he sees you naked every day. It's one thing to watch it day in and day out while you're around, but it's quite another to have intimate conversations when you're in a public place where you're not around.

This can be a real secret game for the two of you, where the winner wins a portion of excellent oral sex. Its rules are simple: everyone completes the task by taking pictures of themselves in a public toilet and the winner is the one who does it more depraved and "dirty". This simple fun, which has a good aphrodisiac effect, will be useful for both a woman and her man.

You can tease your partner with the anticipation of the upcoming evening, describing your desires and sexual fantasies, so that he will return home "warm".

In addition, you can connect your imagination and incline a man to a "dirty" sex chat, describing how you want to taste his sperm and enjoy the feeling of wrapping his hot penis with your lips. You don't need to invent lengthy and exotic opuses – men only need complete frankness and the simplest words.

Make oral sex a real adventure will help and unusual places where the risk of being accidentally "caught in the act" increases. For example, you can show up to your beloved at work and go alone with him in the office toilet, give him a Blowjob in the Elevator or just somewhere in nature, where he did not expect to run into your raging libido.

First, it helps to diversify your sex life and make it clear to the man that you still feel a strong attraction to him. Secondly, this is a great opportunity to occupy not only the partner's bed, but also his thoughts. He doesn't need to fantasize about "bad girls" if he lives under the same roof as one of them. Finally, feeling the indomitable sexual desire of a man, you will gradually learn to enjoy it yourself, even if you previously did not like to do a Blowjob.

Of course, if you are hotly promising something to your partner, you must understand that it will have to be implemented. Otherwise, you risk causing disappointment and even resentment in the soul of a loved one. So, don't promise anything you're not going to do. And if you are not too hot in bed, then start small, so as not to overdo it with "dirty" games.

By the way, I want to mention an interesting fun that one of my long-time patients once told me about. I admit honestly – I even could not resist, and several times played this game with my wife. To say that we both liked it is to say nothing.

The meaning of this game is as follows: you are both locked in different rooms of the house with the phone in your hands, dressed in an equal number of clothes. Each in turn asks the other a frank question, and the other tries to guess the correct answer. For example: "Guess where I'd like to have sex with you right now?" If the partner makes a mistake, they take off one of their things and send a photo of their body to your phone as proof. The first person to be naked loses. He leaves his room and goes to the partner's room to perform his punishment (Blowjob or cunnilingus).

Such erotic games can be invented a great many, but they all make you feel one thing -

the anticipation of future sex, which in itself gives a sense of pleasant tension.

If you were to ask me, as a sex therapist, whether such games actually work, I would say that they certainly do. All this not only brings two people closer to each other and allows you to feel mutual sexual attraction, but also prepares the body of a woman to receive pleasure from the most insignificant touches of a man or to experience the pleasure of a Blowjob made to him.

11. Rule nine: no pain

In theory, every woman understands that oral sex should bring a man only pleasure and pleasant sensations. However, this is only in theory. In fact, inexperienced mistresses very often in a fit of passion do not just cause the partner pain, but also believe that they are evidence of their hot nature.

In fact, no man will like it if during a Blowjob sharp female teeth go into his skin, or even if they just pass casually. The penis is a place of special sensitivity, and "work" with it is supposed to be smooth, gentle and with due care.

Any movement in the area of the male penis should be careful and not sharp, because no lover will thank you if you mercilessly pull his penis with your hand or lips. A gentle Blowjob is the perfect Blowjob, and even as you build up the pace, your movements should remain gliding and smooth.

When starting oral sex, immediately hide your teeth by pulling your lips inside your mouth. It is necessary to grasp the head of the male member in this way, avoiding contact of the teeth with the skin of the partner. Because this is fraught with serious danger – you can accidentally catch the bridle with your teeth, located under the man's head. And then you will not escape her injuries: blood will appear, the thin skin may break, and the partner will remain sad and dissatisfied.

A good mistress will not allow her man to suffer in any way during oral sex, so she will be careful and gentle, helping him relax.

If you are still new to oral sex and are not convinced that you can do everything right without causing pain to your partner, try practicing on a peeled banana. This I say not as a sexologist, but as an ordinary man. Peel the ripe fruit and cover your teeth with your lips, moisten them by licking them. Lower your lips to the top of the banana and, squeezing them into a tight but gentle ring, slide first down and then up, repeating the movements. If you do everything correctly, there will be no traces on the surface of the banana. If you act carelessly, the soft skin of the banana will leave marks and furrows. This means that you will have to learn to do Blowjob correctly and be more gentle.

In addition to the fact that you need to make sure that your teeth do not scratch the sensitive skin of the male penis and do not tear the bridle (sometimes it bleeds even after diligent vaginal sex), you should pay attention to the degree of circumference of the penis with your lips. If you hold it tight enough, the effect of oral sex will significantly decrease. A man likes to feel the compression on the head – from this tight slip comes the feeling of sexual pleasure.

But it is also not necessary to approach this issue too zealously, since the partner's member is a zone susceptible to careless movements. If anything, it's better to wrap your lips around the penis not tightly enough than too tightly. Since it is in the latter case that the risk of injury to the tender area with suddenly slipped teeth increases.

Increase the degree of circumference of the penis with your lips as the partner's sexual tension increases. At first, these are light, barely perceptible gliding movements. Then the lips become tighter and the pace of movement increases. If you feel that a man is ready to feel sexual discharge and ejaculation is just around the corner, then it makes sense to squeeze the head of the penis a little harder with your lips, using the tongue as well.

And remember this: the more moisture there is in the process of oral sex, the better. A high degree of sliding helps to feel high-quality sexual experiences, while a Blowjob "on dry", although it will help the partner to finish faster, will not make an indelible impression on him. Therefore, in certain situations, it makes sense to use a special lubricant for oral sex for the effect of easy sliding. By the way, it will also help to get rid of the unpleasant taste of male lubricant in the mouth, if nature has rewarded you with a squeamish temperament and hypersensitive tongue papillae.

To increase the degree of pleasant sensations during a Blowjob, an unusual temperature will also help, as I have already mentioned in previous chapters. Only if it was cold there, it was warm here. Don't know how to surprise your loved one and make oral sex a little more original? Then drink a cup of hot tea a few minutes before you start oral sex. The increased temperature in the oral cavity will almost certainly excite your partner, because it will be an unusual and new sensation for him.

And don't forget about your tongue – it also plays a huge role when it comes to high-quality Blowjob. First, this speech organ is able to increase the degree of circumference of the penis by pressing it tightly to the upper lip. Secondly, if you have tired lips and unpleasant aching muscles of the cheeks, for a few minutes give yourself a break, completely relaxing your mouth and using your tongue at this time.

When the partner reaches ejaculation, try to restrain the urge to spit out the sperm, even if you do not like the taste of it. Such carelessness can easily offend a man. If you can't bear to keep the partner's seed in your mouth, go to the trick: after the man finishes, continue to slide your lips slowly and unhurriedly for another forty seconds, then relax them to lick the penis. The semen will flow out on the penis itself, but it will not look like you are spitting it out. Some men find this picture especially depraved and "dirty", and they like it very much.

12. Rule ten: do it if you don't know how

If you have no idea how to improve your "oral art" and give your favorite partner a pleasant experience, then use the ready-made step-by-step instructions described below. It is universal and suitable for most couples, fully satisfying the sexual need of a man.

First, put your partner on the bed, without removing his pants and underwear. Let him lie on his back. Slowly climb on top of him and just as slowly get rid of your clothes first.

Still not touching the man and still sitting on his thighs, play a little with your own body: stroke your Breasts and slide your fingers over the nipples, and then gently lower your hands and slightly masturbate so that the partner can see it clearly.

Feeling sexual tension, unbutton the fly of the man's trousers and carefully pull the clothes down. Put one hand in his underpants and stroke his pubis, lightly pressing on the groin area.

In a circular motion, caress his testicles, still avoiding the penis. Only when it fully comes to "combat readiness", slightly squeeze it with your palm, pulling the head.

Pull your partner's underwear off while still sitting on top of him. Lean forward and caress the skin of his belly with your lips and tongue, slowly sinking lower.

Lick the penis, starting from the bottom, until you get to the head. Then wrap your lips around it, moving easily and without exerting much pressure.

Next, make the girth a little tighter, sliding about half of the penis. Put one hand on the base of your partner's penis, wrapping it around the point where it goes to the pubic area. Move your hand in time with your lip movements, increasing the tempo constantly, but slowly.

Put your other hand between your partner's legs and play with his testicles a little. Do it carefully and gently. To improve the pleasant sensations for a while, tear your lips from your partner's penis and lick his testicles, trying to take each in turn in your mouth and gently sucking them.

At the same time, try to massage the partner's buttocks with the other hand, first moistening the edges of your fingers with saliva or oral sex lubricant. If the man does not mind, stroke his anus, slightly pressing on it.

Go back to the penis, this time increasing both the degree of pressing of the lips and the pace with which you move up and down. With one hand, continue to move in time with the base of the penis, and with the other, caress the partner's anal opening.

If a man shows a desire to caress you in response, change your position, turning your back to him and remaining on top. So, he will get the opportunity to play with your genitals or engage in cunnilingus. If you want a response to sexual discharge, help your partner understand this: let him penetrate your vagina with his fingers or suck your clitoris.

To delay the time of ejaculation, watch the behavior of the man. In the event that his penis begins to throb, stop oral sex and wait ten to fifteen seconds. Sometimes this is necessary if you want to experience an orgasm at the same time.

As soon as the partner begins to ejaculate, increase the force of compression of the penis with your lips, trying not to show too much zeal and not to hurt him. Try to put the penis as deep as possible into the mouth opening.

After the partner finishes, do not rush to unclench your lips. Wait till the male penis does not stop the pulsation, however, weaken the movement and make them easy gliding.

To give the partner a special pleasure, you can swallow his sperm or go to the trick I described above, without offending his feelings (many men negatively perceive spitting sperm partner).

Of course, this is just a rough guide to action. After all, each individual couple has their own special sexual preferences and it is always better to listen to the desires of their partner.

Finally, I want to note that men whose partners are regularly satisfied with oral sex usually consider themselves happier and more successful than men who are denied oral sex for one reason or another.

In addition, if you plan to start a family with this partner in the future and give birth to children, frequent Blowjob will avoid severe bouts of toxicosis or, at least, reduce the risk of gestosis of pregnant women in the future, because the female body will learn to recognize the protein of men.

Well, the main advice, as a sexologist, will be simple and concise: love your men and try to be the best mistresses for them. That's the whole secret of family happiness.